D1220782

Life & Death

Also by Robert Creeley

POETRY

For Love • *Words* • *The Charm* • *Pieces*
A Day Book • *Hello: A Journal* • *Later*
Collected Poems: 1945–1975 • *Mirrors*
Memory Gardens • *Selected Poems*
Windows • *Echoes*

FICTION

The Gold Diggers • *The Island*
Presences • *Mabel: A Story*
Collected Prose

DRAMA

Listen

ESSAYS

A Quick Graph: Collected Notes & Essays
Was That a Real Poem & Other Essays
Collected Essays
Autobiography
Tales Out of School

ANTHOLOGIES AND SELECTIONS

The Black Mountain Review 1954–1957
New American Story (with Donald M. Allen)
The New Writing in the U.S.A. (with Donald M. Allen)
Selected Writings of Charles Olson
Whitman: Selected Poems
The Essential Burns
Charles Olson, *Selected Poems*

Robert Creeley
Life & Death

A NEW DIRECTIONS BOOK

ACKNOWLEDGMENTS
   The author would like to acknowledge the generous support of a Lila Wallace–Reader's Digest Fund Writers' Award in the writing of the poems in this collection.
   Grateful acknowledgment is given for permission to quote from Laurence Binyon's translation of Dante, *Purgatorio*, XVIII, 139–145 (by permission of The Society of Authors, on behalf of the Laurence Binyon Estate), and from Wallace Stevens's "Anecdote of the Jar," copyright 1923 and renewed 1951 by Wallace Stevens in *The Collected Poems of Wallace Stevens* (by permission of Alfred A. Knopf, Inc.).
   Grateful acknowledgment is also made to the editors and publishers of magazines in which some of the poems in this book first appeared: *2River View, Arshile, Boxkite, Conjunctions, Crayon, Exquisite Corpse, Gas, Grand Street, "I am a Child," Longhouse, Notre Dame Review, Pharos, University of Durham Library Journal, Valentine.* Thanks too to the publishers of books and pamphlets in which many of the poems also appeared: *The Dogs of Auckland* (Meow Press, 1996), *Edges* (collaboration with Alex Katz; Peter Blum Edition, 1997), *Histoire de Florida* (Ferriss Editions, 1996), *Loops* (Nadja, 1995). Thanks as well to the Maryland Institute of Art's Black Square Press for its broadside of "Echo" (printed by Les Ferris, arranged by John Yau) and to Ben Friedlander of Channel 500 at the State University of New York at Buffalo for its broadside of "Help." And special thanks to the Gagosian Gallery for three collaborations with Francesco Clemente: *Life & Death* (with the Grenfell Press, 1994), *There* (1994), and *Anamorphosis* (1997).

Manufactured in the United States of America
New Directions Books are printed on acid-free paper
First published clothbound by New Directions in 1998
Published simultaneously in Canada by Penguin Books Canada Limited

LIBRARY OF CONGRESS CATALOGING IN PUBLICATION DATA
Creeley, Robert, 1926–
Life & Death / Robert Creeley.
p.   cm.
Includes the previously published Life & death and new poems.
Includes index.
ISBN 0-8112-1384-6 (acid-free paper)
I. Title.
PS3505.R43L44   1998
811'.54—dc21   97-45805
                                                                CIP

New Directions Books are published for James Laughlin
by New Directions Publishing Corporation,
80 Eighth Avenue, New York 10011

Contents

for Pen, Will and Hannah

I

HISTOIRE DE FLORIDA

HISTOIRE DE FLORIDA

You're there
still behind
the mirror,
brother face.

Only yesterday
you were younger,
now you
look old.

Come out
while there's still time
left
to play.

•

Waking, think of sun through
compacted tree branches,
the dense
persistent light.

Think of heaven,
home,
a heart of gold,
old song of friend's

dear love and all
the faint world it
reaches to,
it wants.

•

3

Out over that piece of water
where the sound is, the place
it loops round on the map from
the frontal ocean and makes a
spit of land this sits on, here, flat,
filled with a patent detritus left
from times previous whatever
else was here before become
now brushy conclave thick with
hidden birds, nimble, small lizards.

●

Whatever, whatever.
Wherever, what-
ever, whenever— It won't
be here anymore—
What one supposes
dead is, but what a simple ending,
pain, fear, unendurable
wrenched division, breakdown
of presumed function, truck's broken
down again, no one left
to think of it, fix it, walk on.
Will one fly away on angel wings,
rise like a feather, lift
in the thin air— But again returned,
preoccupied, he counts his life
like cash in emptying pockets.
Somebody better help him.

●

Remember German artist
(surely "conceptual" or
"happenings") ate himself,
cut bits from his body
on stage while audience
watched, it went well
for awhile. But then
he did something wrong
and bled to death.
*The art is long
to learn, life short.*

•

It must be anecdotal,
sudden sights along the so-called way,
Bunting's advice that David Jones
when he first met him had moved but once
in adult life and then only
when the building burned down
to a place across the street.
They were having tea
when abruptly Jones got up,
went to an easel at the far end of the room
whereon a sheet of drawing paper
with, in his immaculate script, a 't,'
added an 'h' to say,
"I'll have the 'e' by Monday!"
Affections flood me,
love lights light in like eyes...

•

Your two eyes will me
suddenly slay…
Such echoes
of heaven on earth

in mind as if
such *a glass* through which
seen *darkly*
such reflected truth.

What words, then,
if you love me,
what *beauty*
not to be *sustained*

will separate
finally
dancer
from *dance.*

●

Sun meantime
shining

just now (now) a
yellow slid

oblong
patch (light)

from wide
window

●

But don't get physical
with me. Topper, or the Cheshire cat
whose head could appear grinning
in the tree. Could appear
in the window.
Could see
in the dark.

    •

You still think
death is a subject,
or a place
in time?

Like halving the distance,
the arrow that never gets there.
I died and came back again
to the very spot I'd seemingly

left from, in a Raj-like hotel,
Calcutta, 1944. From lunch of prawns
got up and went to my room,
an hour later dimly recall was on hands and knees

crawling to quondam toilet
to vomit and shit, then must
have collapsed completely en route back
to the bed and a long time later heard

voice (hotel doctor's, they told me)
saying, must get him to hospital,
he can't die here. But I'd gone away
down long faint space of path

or up, or simply out,
was moving away into a reassuring distance
of somewhere
(heaven? I don't think so—

My temperature was 96 etc.
Délires! Whatever— Wherever
had come to, gone to,
I wasn't there.

　　　•

Leary at Naropa for celebration
of Kerouac I remember saying, it's dumb to die—
It's for squares! Gregory
thought it a dumb thing to say to the young.

Was it metaphysical?
Did he mean something else.
Whether with drugs or not,
be rid of such terminal dependence?

As if, and why not,
closure were just fact
of a clogged pipe,
all coming to naught?

Get it out.
Open up?
—But the syntax would be,
"What proceeds and what follows,"

in Pound's phrase,
like a river,
the emptying sounds
of paradise.

•

In pajamas still
late morning sun's at my back
again through the window,
figuring mind still, figuring place
I am in, which is me,
solipsistic, a loop yet moving, moving,
with these insistent proposals
of who, where, when,
what's out there, what's in,
what's the so-called art of anything,
hat, house, hand, head, heart, and so on,
quickly banal. Always reflections.
No light on the water, no clouds lifting, bird's flap taking off—
Put the food in mouth, feel throat swallowing,
warmth is enough.

Emotions recollected in tranquillity…
which is what?
Feelings now are not quiet, daughter's threatened
kidneys, sister's metal knee replacement, son's
vulnerable neighborhood friendships, Penelope's social
suitors, whom I envy, envy.
Age. Age.
Locked in my mind,
my body, toes broken, skin
wrinkling up, look to the ceiling
where, through portals of skylight,
two rectangular glass boxes in the stained wood,
the yellow light comes, an outside is evident.
There is no irony, no patience.

There is nothing to wait for
that isn't here, and it will happen.
Happiness is thus lucky.
Not I but the wind that blows through me.

●

Another day. Drove to beach,
parked the car on the edge of the road
and walked up on the wooden ramp provided,
then stopped just before the steps down to the sand
and looked out at the long edge of the surf, the sun glitter,
the backdrop of various condominiums and cottages,
the usual collective of people, cars, dogs and birds.
It was sweet to see company,
and I was included.

Yet Crusoe—
Whose mind was that, Defoe's?
Like Kafka's *Amerika,* or Tom Jones come to London.
Or Rousseau, or Odysseus—
One practices survival
much as we did when kids and would head for the woods
with whatever we could pilfer or elders gave us,
doughnuts, cookies, bread—
Even in one's own terror,
one is proud of a securing skill.

But what so turned things
to pain, and if Mandelstam's poem is found scratched
on cell wall in the gulag
by anonymous hand,
and that's all of either we know—

Why isn't that instance of the same
side of world Robinson Crusoe comes to,
footprint on sand a terror,
person finally discovered an adversary
he calls "Friday,"
who then he learns "to be good"—

But I wouldn't, I can't
now know or resolve
when it all became so singular,
when first that other door closed,
and the beach and the sunlight faded,
surf's sounds grew faint, and one's thoughts took over,
bringing one home.

•

At a dinner
in Kuala Lumpur

where I was the guest
together with a sewerage expert

had most recently worked in Saudi Arabia
where drainage was the problem,

and here it was the same,
we talked of conveniences,

shopping malls, suburbs,
and what had been hauled over

from stateside habit,
the bars and people,

while just down the street
was what the Kuala Lumpurians called

The Backside of Hell,
a short alley of small doorways

and open stalls.
They said here anything was possible.

Meantime in our hotel lobby
they had dyed some chicks a weird bluish pink

and put them in a little cage
out front for Easter.

It's always one world
if you can get there.

●

HISTOIRE DE FLORIDA

Old persons swinging their canted metal detectors,
beach's either end out of sight beyond the cement block highrises,
occasional cars drifting by in the lanes provided,
sheer banks of the dunes bulkheaded by bulldozers,
there a few cars backed up, parked.
People walk by or stretch out on cots,
turning in the sun's heat, tanning.

The line of the surf at some distance, small,
the white edge of breakers where the surfers cluster.
On the far horizon, east, is bulk of a freighter,
to the north, tower of a lighthouse across the inlet.
Back of it all the town sells the early tourists,
the stores filling with elderly consumers.
The old are gathering for an old-time ritual.

One knows that in the waters hereabouts, in a particular spring,
Ponce de Leon staggered in so as *to live forever.*
But poisoned with infection from a local's arrow
and conned by the legend of eternal youth,
he'd led all his people into a bloody cul-de-sac
and ended himself being fed to alligators
ate him skin and bones, leaving no trace.

So it may be we all now look
for where the first of these old folks went down,
seeing his own face in the placid creek,
hearing the far-off murmur of the surf,
feeling his body open in the dark,
the warmth of the air, the odor of the flowers,
the eternal maiden waiting soft in her bower.

•

This is the lovely time
of late afternoon
when the sun comes in
through slatted blinds.

The large glass panes
show streaks in the dust.
Bushy laurel's green leaves
turn golden beyond.

I hear plane pass over
high in the sky,
see flowers in vase tremble
with table's movement.

Company's become
room's quiet hum.
This hanging silence
fills with sound.

•

Determined reading
keeps the mind's attention
off other things, fills
the hole in symbolic stocking

now that Xmas approaches—
a truck through proverbial night,
the buzzes, roars, of silence
I hear here

all alone.
Poor, wee Robbie!
Flickering light in small window,
meager head and heart in hand,

I recall William Bartram
somewhere in 18th century Florida
on night not unlike this one,
after he'd hauled his skiff up on shore,

then laid down, so he wrote,
to sleep when sudden uproar,
thumpings, bangings, poundings!
all seeming very close,

awakened him to possibility
he was going to die.
But, stalwart,
checked it out

to find an alligator had clambered up
and over the gunnels of his boat
to get dead fish Bartram had left inside—
and all was finally well.

He drew great pictures of "the natives,"
looking like quaint
18th century English persons
in beguiling states of undress.

He had a heart I wish I had.
My car is parked in the driveway.
My door is locked. I do not want
to go outside.

•

What was resistance.
How come to this.
Wasn't body's package
obvious limit,

could I fly,
could I settle,
could I even
be I...

And for what want,
watching man die
on tv in Holland, wife
sitting by.

She said, "He's
going off alone
for the first time
in our lives."

He told her,
"to the stars, to the
Milky Way,"
relaxed, and was gone.

What is Florida
to me or me
to Florida except
so defined.

•

You've left a lot out
Being in doubt
you left
it out

Your mother
Aunt Bernice
in Nokomis
to the west

and south (?)
in trailer park
Dead now for years
as one says

You've left
them out
David
your son

Your friend
John
You've left
them out

You thought
you were writing
about
what you felt

You've left it out
Your love
your life
your home

your wife
You've
left her
out

No one is one
No one's alone
No world's that small
No life

You left it out

•

The shell was the apparent
inclusion, that *another* might be here.
Form, the provision,
what one took, or didn't,

from another. What form
did it take,
what way
did it matter?

My mind was a supermarket
or a fading neighborhood store.
I couldn't find anything anymore,
or just didn't have it.

I is another...
and another, another,
blocks fading, streets
fading, into an emptying distance.

Who tore it down.
Where was it, what
was it. Where do you think
you left it?

My mother in Nokomis,
Aunt Bernice in Nokomis,
David in Sarasota,
Mary Ann, Cecelia, Rebecca

in Sarasota, John in
Sarasota, or Long Island,
Pen, Will and Hannah,
Helen, in Buffalo—

how use *them* simply as loci,
points of reference,
who made me substance?
Sarah calls to say she is pregnant

and *that* is a delicious sound—
like the music Caliban hears
sometimes in Prospero's cell
surrounding him.

•

Rise into the air and look down
and see it there, the pendant form of it,
the way it goes out, alone, into an ocean,

the end of a pattern suddenly extended
to cover, in itself, the western reach, the gulf close beyond.
Its fragile surfaces are watery, swamps to the south,

to the north where its population gathers in flat cities,
sandy wastes, oaks, palmetto, laurel, pine and (for me)
an unidentified particularity more seen, felt, than known.

Perhaps the whole place is a giant pier out
into nothing, or into all that is other, all else.
Miles and miles of space are here in unexpected senses,

sky washed with clouds, changing light, long sunsets
sinking across water and land, air that freshens, intimate.
Endless things growing, all horizontal, an edge, a rise only of feet

above the sea's surface, or the lakes, the ponds, the rivers,
all out, nothing that isn't vulnerable, no depths, no rooted senses
other than the actual fabric of roots, skin of survivals.

•

I placed a jar in Tennessee,
In Florida I placed a jar
And round it was, upon a hill...
And all around it grew important air

... And tall and of a port in air.
It was my first time there
It took dominion everywhere.
and I was far from home and scared

The jar was gray and bare.
in Florida, like nothing else
... Like nothing else in Tennessee.
In Florida. Like nothing else.

II
OLD POEMS, ETC.

ECHO

of the nameless
breather"— The brother,
sister, of the faceless
now adamant body, all
still unsaid, unfledged,
unrecognized until
death all so sudden
comes for the people
and we are one
in this covenant, all the nameless,
those still breathing,
all brothers, sisters,
mothers, fathers,
just a piece of the real,
the fading action, one after one
this indifferent, inexorable, *bitter*
affliction strikes down—

CREDO

Creo que si... I believe
it will rain
tomorrow... I believe
the son of a bitch

is going into the river...
I believe *All men are*
created equal —By your
leave a leafy

shelter over the exposed
person— *I'm a*
believer creature
of habit but without

out there a void of
pattern older
older the broken
pieces no longer

salvageable bits
but incommensurate
chips yet must
get it back together.

In God we
trust emptiness privilege
will not not *perish*
perish *from this earth*—

In particular echo
of inside pushes
at edges all these years
collapse in slow motion.

The will to believe,
the will to be good,
the will to want
a way out—

Humanness, like
you, man. Us—pun
for once beyond reflective
mirror of brightening prospect?

I believe what it was
was a hope it could be
somehow what it was
and would so continue.

A plank to walk out on,
fair enough. *Jump!* said the pirate.
Believe me if all
those endearing young charms...

Here, as opposed to there,
even in confusions there seems
still a comfort,
still a faith.

I'd as lief
not leave, not
go away, not
not believe.

I believe in belief...
All said, whatever I can think of
comes from there,
goes there.

As it gets now impossible
to say, it's your hand
I hold to, still
your hand.

A FEELING

However far
I'd gone,
it was still
where it had all begun.

What stayed
was a feeling of difference,
the imagination
of adamant distance.

Some time,
place,
some other way it was,
the turned face

one loved,
remembered,
had looked for
wherever,

it was all now
outside
and in
was oneself again

except there too
seemed nowhere,
no air,
nothing left clear.

SILENCE

I can't speak so
simply of whatever
was then
the fashion

of silence
everyone's— Blue
expansive morning
and in

the lilac bush just
under window
farm house
spaces all

the teeming chatter
of innumerable birds—
I'd lie quiet
trying

to go to sleep late
evenings in summer
such buzzes settling
twitters

of birds— The relatives
in rooms underneath
me murmuring—
Listened hard to catch

faint edges of sounds
through blurs of a fading
spectrum now out
there forever.

OLD STORY

Like kid on float
of ice block sinking
in pond the field had made
from winter's melting snow

so wisdom accumulated
to disintegrate
in conduits of brain
in neural circuits faded

while gloomy muscles shrank
mind padded the paths
its thought had wrought
its habits had created

till like kid afloat
on ice block broken
on or inside the thing it stood
or was forsaken.

GIVEN

Can you recall
distances, odors,
how far from the one
to the other, stalls

for the cows,
the hummocks one jumped to,
the lawn's webs,
touch, taste of specific

doughnuts, cookies,
what a pimple was
and all such way
one's skin was a place—

Touch, term, turn of curious fate.
Who can throw a ball,
who draw a face,
who knows how.

THE MIRROR

Seeing is believing.
Whatever was thought or said,

these persistent, inexorable deaths
make faith as such absent,

our humanness a question,
a disgust for what we are.

Whatever the hope,
here it is lost.

Because we coveted our difference,
here is the cost.

PICTURES

The little bed
they put me in
with the grim pictures
facing in

The freak of death
for one so young
The fear of cuts
blood leaking out

The sudden abandon
of pleasure, summer
The seasons
The friends

One fall evening driving
in car with teacher
fellow student girl
sitting beside me

on way back from
first play seen
in Boston "Macbeth"
Why did they kill them

Why was my body
flooded
with tension
my small cock stiff

LOOPS

The other who I'd be
never the same as me
no way to step outside and see
more than some penitence of memory—

As day fades to the dust-filled light
in the window in the back wall beyond sight
where I can feel the coming night
like an old friend who sets all to rights—

In the constrictions of this determined scribble
despite slipping thought's wobble
the painful echoing senses of trouble
I've caused others and cannot end now—

Boxed in a life too late to know other
if there was ever any other
but fact of a lost tether
kept the other still somehow there—

To try now to say goodbye
as if one could try to die
in some peculiar mind
wanted to step outside itself for a last try—

To be oneself once and for all
to look through the window and see the wall
and want no more
of anything at all beyond.

THINKING

Grandmother I'd thought
to have called all together
night before dying
in the bed at the stairs' top

when I'd walked
with blackened sky
overhead the storm
and the lightning flashing

back past the Montagues
from the ice pond
and rotting icehouse
held the common pigeons

wanting all to go forward as ever
with grandmother
confidently ill I thought
giving last orders to us all

my mother the elder,
thus to take care
of sister Bernice and younger brother—
did she say as I thought,

I'm tired now
and roll over—
Was it book I'd read
said death's so determined—

whilst grandma crying
out to us
to come and help her
shook, coughed and died?

GOODBYE

Now I recognize
it was always me
like a camera
set to expose

itself to a picture
or a pipe
through which the water
might run

or a chicken
dead for dinner
or a plan
inside the head

of a dead man.
Nothing so wrong
when one considered
how it all began.

It was Zukofsky's
Born very young into a world
already very old...
The century was well along

when I came in
and now that it's ending,
I realize it won't
be long.

But couldn't it all have been
a little nicer,
as my mother'd say. Did it
have to kill everything in sight,

did right always have to be so wrong?
I know this body is impatient.
I know I constitute only a meager voice and mind.
Yet I loved, I love.

I want no sentimentality.
I want no more than home.

"PRESENT (PRESENT)…"

"What is Williams' (Raymond's) tome…"
Where have all the flowers gone?

I put them right here on the table…
No one's been here but for Mabel.

God, my mind is slipping cogs,
gaps of pattern, mucho fog…

Yet I know whatever I
can ever think of ere I die,

'twill be in my head alone
that the symbiotic blur has formed—

to make no "we" unless "they" tell "us"
"you" is "me" and "I" is nameless.

"Tom" is wrong? "I" is right?
Is this the point at which "we" fight?

Us was never happy we,
all that's ever left is me.

Past is what I can't forget,
where the flowers got to yet—

Mabel's face, my mother's hands,
clouds o'erhead last year at Cannes,

Kenneth Koch's reaction when
we told him once at 3 AM

he should marry Barbara Epstein,
loosen up and have some fun.

"I remember, I remember—"
Memory, the great pretender,

says it happened, thinks it was,
this way, that way, just because

it was in my head today…
Present (present) passed away.

HELP

Who said you didn't want
to keep what you've got
and would help the other guy
share the bulging pot

of goodies you got
just by being bought
on time by the plot
wouldn't give you a dime

sick or not
you've got to stay well
if you want to buy time
for a piece of the lot

where you all can hang out
when you aren't sick in bed
blood running out
bones broken down

eyes going blind
ears stuffed up
stomach a bloat
you battered old goat

but nothing to keep up
no payments to make
no insurance is fine
when you plan to die

when you don't mind the wait
if you can't stand up
and all the others are busy
still making money.

A VALENTINE FOR PEN

I love you, says the clock, paradoxically silent, watching
through the night with red eyes. *I love you,* says the long
wooden table across from the wide bed with the bookcase
upright beside it, the black lamp arching over, the old computer
waiting for its work. *I love you, I love you,* the echoes, reaches
of the tall room, the hanging pictures, the catalogs, clothes, the
cats securely sleeping on the disheveled old couch, the pulled up
small rug put over its cushions, all say it, the enclosing dear room,
the balcony above which opens at each end to bedrooms of the
children, *I love you,* says Hannah's ample particular heart, says
Will's wide responsive heart, says each resonance of every sweet
morning's opening, here said, again and again, *I love you.*

BREATH

for Szusan Rothenberg

Breath as a braid, a tugging
squared circle, "steam, vapour—
an odorous exhalation,"
breaks the heart when it
stops. It is the living, the
moment, sound's curious
complement to *breadth,*
brethren, "akin to BREED…"
And what see, feel, know as
"the air inhaled and exhaled
in respiration," in substantial
particulars—as a horse?

●

Not language paints,
pants, patient, a pattern.
A horse (here *horses*) is
seen. Archaic in fact,
the word alone
presumes a world,
comes willy-nilly thus back
to where it had all begun.
These horses *are,* they reflect
on us, their seeming ease
a gift to all that lives,
and looks and breathes.

FOUR DAYS IN VERMONT

Window's tree trunk's predominant face
a single eye-leveled hole where limb's torn off
another larger contorts to swell growing in around
imploding wound beside a clutch of thin twigs
hold to one two three four five six dry twisted
yellowish brown leaves flat against the other
grey trees in back stick upright then the glimpse
of lighter still greyish sky behind the close
welted solid large trunk with clumps of grey-green
lichen seen in boxed glass squared window back
of two shaded lamps on brown chiffonier between
two beds echo in mirror on far wall of small room.

•

(for Maggie)

Most, death left a hole
a place where she'd been
An emptiness stays
no matter what or who
No law of account not
There but for the
grace of God go I
Pain simply of want
last empty goodbye
Put hand on her head
good dog, good dog
feel her gone.

•

Tree adamant looks in
its own skin mottled with growths
its stubborn limbs
stick upright parallel
wanting to begin again
looking for sun in the sky
for a warmer wind
to walk off pull up
roots and move
to Boston be a table
a chair a house
a use a final fire.

•

What is truth *firm (as a tree)*
Your faith your trust your loyalty
Agrees with the facts makes
world consistent plights a troth
is friendly sits in the common term
All down the years all seasons all sounds
all persons saying things conforms confirms
Contrasts with "war equals confusion" *(worse)*
But *Dichtung und Wahrheit*? "Wahr-" is
very ("Verily I say unto you...") A compact now
Tree lights with the morning though *truth* be an oak
This is a maple, is a *tree*, as a very truth firm.

•

Do I rootless shift
call on the phone
daughter's warm voice
her mother's clear place
Is there wonder here
has it all gone inside
myself become subject
weather surrounds
Do I dare go out
be myself specific
be as the tree
seems to look in.

•

Breeze at the window
lifts the light curtains
Through the dark a light
across the faint space
Warmth out of season
fresh wash of ground
out there beyond
sits here waiting
For whatever time comes
herein welcome
Wants still
truth of the matter.

•

Neighbor's light's still on
outside above stoop
Sky's patchy breaks
of cloud and light
Around is a valley
over the hill
to the wide flat river
the low mountains secure
Who comes here with you
sits down in the room
what have you left
what's now to do.

•

Soon going day wanders on
and still tree's out there waiting
patient in time like a river and
truth a simple apple reddened
by frost and sun is found
where one had left it in time's company
No one's absent in mind None gone
Tell me the *truth* I want to say
Tell me all you know Will we live
or die As if the world were apart
and whatever tree seen were only here apparent
Answers, live and die. Believe.

THE DOGS OF AUCKLAND

1.

Curious, coming again here,
where I hadn't known where I was ever,

following lead of provident strangers,
around the corners, out to the edges,

never really looking back but kept
adamant forward disposition, a Christian

self-evident resolve, small balloon of purpose
across the wide ocean, friends, relations,

all left behind. Each day the sun rose, then set.
It must be the way life is, like they say, a story

someone might have told me. I'd have listened.
Like the story Murray recalled by Janet Frame

in which a person thinks to determine what's most necessary
to life, and strips away legs, arms, trunk—

to be left with a head, more specifically, a brain,
puts it on the table, and a cleaning woman comes in,

sees the mess and throws it into the dustbin.
Don't think of it, just remember? Just then there was a gorgeous

light on the street there, where I was standing, waiting
for the #005 bus at the end of Queen Street, just there on Customs,

West—dazzling sun, through rain. "George is/gorgeous/
George is..." So it begins.

2.

Almost twenty years ago I fled my apparent life, went off
into the vast Pacific, though it was only miles and miles

in a plane, came down in Auckland Airport, was met by Russell Haley—
and he's still here with Jean, though they've moved

to the east coast a few hours away, and Alan Loney is here
as ever my friend. And Wystan, whose light I might see there

across the bay, blinking. And Alistair Paterson is here with a thirty-
four-foot boat up the harbor—as in comes the crew of *Black Magic*

with the America's Cup, in their yellow slickers, the cars moving down
Queen Street, the crowd there waiting some half million—

in the same dazzling light in which I see tiny, seemingly dancing figures
at the roof's edge of the large building back of the square, looking
    [down.

How to stay real in such echoes? How be, finally, anywhere the body's
    [got to?
You were with friends, sir? Do you know their address…

They walk so fast through Albert Park. Is it my heart causes these
awkward, gasping convulsions? I can mask the grimace with a smile,

can match the grimace with a smile. I can. *I think I can.*
Flooded with flat, unyielding sun, the winter beds of small plants

form a pattern, if one looks, a design. There is Queen Victoria still,
and not far from her the statue of a man. Sit down, sit down.

3. *(for Pen)*

Scale's intimate. From the frame and panes of the fresh white
painted windows in the door, to the deck, second floor, with its

white posts and securing lattice of bars, but nothing, *nothing* that
would ever look like that, just a small porch, below's the garden,

winter sodden, trampoline, dark wet green pad pulled tight, a lemon
tree thick with fruit. And fences, backyards, neighbors surrounding,
    [in

all the sloping, flattened valley with trees stuck in like a kid's picture,
palms, Norfolk pine, stubby ones I can't name, a church spire,
    [brownish

red at the edge of the far hill, also another prominent bald small
    [dome,
both of which catch the late sun and glow there near the head of
    [Ponsonby Road.

The Yellow Bus stops up the street, where Wharf comes into Jervois
    [Road,
off Buller to Bayfield, where we are. I am writing this, sitting at the
    [table,

and love you more and more. When you hadn't yet got here, I set to
    [each morning
to learn "New Zealand" (I thought) as if it were a book simply. I
    [listened to everyone.

Now we go to bed as all, first Will and Hannah, in this rented house,
    [then us,
lie side by side, reading. Then off with the light and to sleep, to slide
    [close up

to one another, sometimes your bottom tucked tight against my belly or
mine lodged snug in your lap. *Sweet dreams, dear heart, till the morning*
    [*comes.*

4·

Back again, still new, from the south
where it's cold now, and people didn't seem to

know what to do, cars sliding, roads blocked with snow,
walk along here through the freshening morning

down the wet street past green plastic garbage bins,
past persistent small flowering bushes, trees. Like the newcomer

come to town, the dogs bark and one on a porch
across from the house where we live makes a fuss

when I turn to go in through the gate. Its young slight
mistress comes out as if in dream, scolds the sad dog,

cuffing it with shadowy hands, then goes back in.
I wonder where sounds go after they've been,

where light once here is now, what, like the joke,
is bigger than life and blue all over, or brown all over,

here where I am. How big my feet seem, how curiously
solid my body. Turning in bed at night with you gone, alone here,

looking out at the greyish dark, I wonder who else is alive.
Now our bus lumbers on up the hill from the stop at the foot of Queen
    [Street—

another late rain, a thick sky—past the laboring traffic when just
    [across
at an intersection there's another bus going by, its windows

papered with dogs, pictures of dogs, all sizes, kinds and colors,
looking real, patient like passengers, who must be behind

sitting down in the seats. Stupid to ask what things mean if it's only
to doubt them. That was a bus going elsewhere? Ask them.

5.

Raining again. Moments ago the sky was a grey lapping pattern
towards the light at the edges still, over Auckland, at the horizon.

It's closed in except for the outline of a darker small cloud
with pleasant, almost lacelike design laid over the lighter sky.

Things to do today. Think of Ted Berrigan, friends absent or dead.
Someone was saying, *you don't really know where you are*

till you move away— "How is it far if you think it." I have still the sense
I've got this body to take care of, a thing someone left me in mind

as it were. Don't forget it. The dogs were there when I went
up to the head of the street to shop for something to eat and a lady,

unaggressively but particular to get there, pushes in to pay for some
    [small items
she's got, saying she wants to get back to her house before the rain.

The sky is pitch-black toward the creek. She's there as I pass with my
    [packages,
she's stopped to peer into some lot has a board enclosure around it,

and there are two dogs playing, bouncing up on each other.
Should I bounce, then, in friendship, against this inquisitive lady,

bark, be playful? One has no real words for that.
Pointless otherwise to say anything she was so absorbed.

6.

I can't call across it, see it as a piece, am dulled with its reflective
    [prospect,
want all of it but can't get it, even a little piece here. Hence the dogs,

"The Dogs of Auckland," who were there first walking along with
    [their company,
seemed specific to given streets, led the way, accustomed.

Nothing to do with sheep or herding, no presence other than one
    [cannily human,
a scale kept the city particular and usefully in proportion.

When I was a kid I remember lifting my foot up carefully, so as to
    [step over
the castle we'd built with blocks. The world here is similar. The sky
    [so vast,

so endless the surrounding ocean. No one could swim it.
It's a basic company we've come to.

They say people get to look like their dogs, and if I could,
I'd have been Maggie, thin long nose, yellowish orange hair,

a frenetic mongrel terrier's delight in keeping it going, eager,
vulnerable, but she's gone. All the familiar stories of the old man

and his constant companion, the dog, Bowser.
My pride that Norman Mailer lists *Bob, Son of Battle*

as a book he valued in youth
as I had also. Warm small proud lonely world.

Coming first into this house, from seemingly nowhere
a large brown amiable dog went bounding in

up the steps in front of us, plunged through various rooms
and out. Farther up the street is one less secure, misshapen,

a bit thin-haired where it's worn, twists on his legs, quite small.
This afternoon I thought he'd come out to greet me, coming home.

He was at the curb as I came down and was headed toward me.
Then he got spooked and barked, running, tail down, for his house.

I could hear all the others, back of the doors, howling,
sounding the painful alarm.

7·

Empty, vacant. Not the outside but in. What you thought was
a place, you'd determined by talk,

and, turning, neither dogs nor people
were there. Pack up the backdrop. Pull down

the staging. Not "The Dogs" but The Dog of Auckland—
Le Chien d'Auckland, c'est moi!

I am the one with the missing head in the gully
Will saw, walking up the tidal creekbed. I am the one

in the story the friend told, of his Newfoundland,
hit by car at Auckland city intersection, crossing on crosswalk,

knocked down first, then run over, the driver
anxious for repairs to his car. I am the Dog.

Open the sky, let the light back in.
Your ridiculous, pinched faces confound me.

Your meaty privilege, lack of distinguishing measure,
skill, your terrifying, mawkish dependence—

You thought for even one moment it was Your World?
Anubis kills!

8.

"Anubis" rhymes with Auckland, says the thoughtful humanist—
at least an "a" begins each word, and from there on it's

only a matter of miles. By now I have certainly noticed
that the dogs aren't necessarily with the people at all, nor are the
    [people

with the dogs. It's the light,
backlit buildings, the huge sense of floating,

platforms of glass like the face
of the one at the edge of Albert Park

reflects (back) the trees, for that charmed
moment all in air. That's where we are.

So how did the dogs get up here, eh?
I didn't even bring myself, much less them.

In the South Island a bull terrier is minding sheep
with characteristic pancake-flat smile.

Meantime thanks, even if now much too late,
to all who move about "down on all fours"

in furry, various coats. Yours was the kind accommodation,
the unobtrusive company, or else the simple valediction of a look.

EDGES

Expectably slowed yet unthinking
of outside when in, or weather
as ever more than there when
everything, anything, will be again

Particular, located, familiar in its presence
and reassuring. The end
of the seeming dream was simply
a walk down from the house through the field.

I had entered the edges, static,
had been walking without attention,
thinking of what I had seen, whatever,
a flotsam of recollections, passive reflection.

My own battered body, clamorous
to roll in the grass, sky looming,
the myriad smells ecstatic, felt insistent prick of things
under its weight, wanted something

Beyond the easy, commodious adjustment
to determining thought, the loss of reasons
to ever do otherwise than comply—
tedious, destructive interiors of mind

As whatever came in to be seen,
representative, inexorably chosen,
then left as some judgment.
Here thought had its plan.

Is it only in dreams
can begin the somnambulistic rapture?
Without apparent eyes?
Just simply looking?

All these things were out there
waiting, innumerable, patient.
How could I name even one enough,
call it only a flower or a distance?

If ever, just one moment, a place
I could be in where all imagination would fade
to a center, wondrous, beyond any way
one had come there, any sense,

And the far-off edges of usual
place were inside. Not even the shimmering
reflections, not one even transient ring
come into a thoughtless mind.

Would it be wrong to say, *the sky is up,*
the ground is down, and out there
is what can never be the same—
what, like music, has gone?

Trees stay outside one's thought.
The water stays stable in its shifting.
The road from here to there continues.
One is included.

Here it all is then—
as if expected,
waited for and found
again.

WON'T IT BE FINE?

At whatever age he was, he was apt with that
"not with a bang but a whimper…" Wiseass little
prick felt himself thus projected an impervious
balloon into history. Or maybe not at all so,

just spooked he had blown it again or been blown
out by old-time time's indifference to anything
wouldn't fit the so-called pattern. I am tired, I am
increasingly crippled by my own body's real wear

and tear, and lend my mind to an obsessional search for
les images des jeunes filles or again not so
young at all with huge tits, or come-hither looks,
or whatever my failing head now projects as desirable.

What was I looking at sunk once full weight onto others,
some of whom I hardly knew or even wanted to, mean-
minded bastard that I was and must perforce continue
to be. God help us all who have such fathers, or lovers,

as I feel myself to have been, be, and think to spend
quiet evenings at home while he (me), or they, plural,
pad the feral passages, still in their bedroom slippers,
never dressing anymore but peering out, distracted,

for the mailman, the fellow with the packages, the persons
having the wrong address, or even an unexpected friend appearing.
"No, I never go out anymore, having all I need right here"—
and looks at his wife, children, the dog, as if they were only

a defense. Because where he has been and is cannot admit them.
He has made a tediously contrived "thing to do today" with
his own thing, short of cutting it off. There is no hope in hope,
friends. If you have friends, be sure you are good to them.

SIGNS

1.

The old ones say, "The peach keeps its fuzz until it dies." It seemed
for years as if one would never grow up, never be the first to say
anything. But time is like a river, rather, a dank, sluggish rush, and
here one is at last as anticipated old on its nether bank. I stand
there bewildered, in my pajamas, shouting, "The stone is an apple
before it's got hard!" *The ground is the bottom of the sky.*

2.

It begins with I stand there. The old ones say, "The speech keeps its
fizz until it dries." For years and years one never grew up, never
first or last. But was like a river rather, a dark whoosh, and there was
at last one old anticipated on the dark bank. *I* stands there in my
pajamas. Shouts, *apple stone hard's got! Hands wrought, God's bought—*
Bodies! The sky is ground at the bottom.

3.

The. Bod. Ies. Han. Ds. God. S. Bough. T.
(Ic. An. *Read.*) Ston. Es. St. And. Sh. Out. T. Here.
Sky. See. Is. At. T. He. Har. Ds.

It was no friend of mine they shot they caught no friend of mine they
sought they thought they fought. Alone on the far bank old now to be there
he ought not...

Ought not.

Got. Bot. (Of) Tom. The Sky. (Of) God. The Eye.
Bot. Tom. Each. Sp. Eech. P. Each. Lies lie.

4.

I cannot tell the truth anymore. I am too old to remember by what right or wrong one was then to be the measure, so as to think that if this, of two, might be down, then that, of one, would be up. The birds make the lovely music just outside the opened windows as we lie there on the freshly made beds in the attractive *chambres des* dispossessed. Or maid or *made.* Make *Mary* dirty man! *This is Hull nor are you out of it,* saith.

5.

"He ate the Hull thing." I lied when I told you I was lying. Clean sheets for dirty bodies, God's dotties, odd's potties. Where's the far bank on the corner of. Neither lip's invitation. I can't see the water for the sky. Each year's a peach, hard, and no friend. Bought or sought or fought or caught. What ever happened to rabbits? Did we finally eat them all?

Sieh' D' Rahm!

I need some "water" at this point
where "sky" meets "ground"
—to lead one reader on,
and so a wandering mind anoint...

6.

Watery disposition. Spongy, rubbery surfaces. Sinking ground. Nowhere one sensible, solid support. Looks up from within the well's depth. Looks out from the edge of the prospect. Down, in. Up, out. Light. Dark. I remember we were sitting on the rock in the clearing. We were standing by the dock near the mooring. Lock of door shutting. Clock's ticking. Walks thinking. Thinner than one was. Aging beginner, sinner. Talks.

7.

You have never had chance to speak of how particularly love mattered in your life, nor of the many ways it so invaded you, chafed, rubbed, itched, "grew wet with desire," long, soft, hard, etc. You were observant of cares in such matters, bulks of person, legs, arms, heads, etc. It's hard to budge the real if it's not your own. *Born very young into a world already very old...* Even spitting it out was often awkward. Seemingly unseemly, uncertain. Curtain. Hide it from view, then, until they've all gone.

8.

What was it friend said? "We are the old ones now!" But that was years ago. Sitting right there where you are. I was. He is. Time's like a rover we'll go no more of. Apple's at bottom of bushel turned to stone. *But I am tired of apples speaking now...* Peaches. Faded speeches. Fuzz turned to screaming sirens and old dead men. Dank river darkened in dusk of dead ends. Hits bottom.

ECHO'S ARROW

for Jackson Mac Low

Were there answers where they were
There where air was everywhere
Time to make impassioned stir
Place to find an answer for

Place to find an answer for
Time to make impassioned stir
There where air was everywhere
Were there answers where they were

OLD POEMS

One wishes the *herd* still wound its way
to mark the end of the departing day
or that the road were *a ribbon of moonlight*
tossed between something cloudy (?) or that *the night*

were still something to be walked in like a lake
or that even a bleak stair *down which the blind*
were *driven* might still prove someone's fate—
and pain and love as always still *unkind.*

My shedding body, skin soft as a much worn
leather glove, head empty as an emptied winter pond,
collapsing arms, hands looking like stubble, rubble,
outside still those barns of my various childhood,

the people I still hold to, mother, my grandfather,
grandmother, my sister, the frames of necessary love,
the ones defined me, told me who I was or what I am
and must now learn to let go of, give entirely away.

There cannot be less of me than there was,
not less of things I'd thought to save, or forgot,
placed in something I lost, or ran after,
saw disappear down a road itself is no longer there.

Pump on, old heart. Stay put, vainglorious blood,
red as the something something.
"Evening comes and comes..." What
was that great poem about *the man against*

the sky just at the top of the hill
with the last of the vivid sun still behind him
and one couldn't tell
whether he now went up or down?

MITCH

Mitch was a classmate
later married extraordinary poet
and so our families were friends
when we were all young
and lived in New York, New Hampshire, France.

He had eyes with whites
above eyeballs looked out
over lids in droll surmise—
"gone under earth's lid" was Pound's phrase,
cancered stomach?

A whispered information over phone,
two friends the past week…,
the one, she says, an eccentric dear woman,
conflicted with son?
Convicted with ground

tossed in, one supposes,
more dead than alive.
Life's done all it could
for all of them.
Time to be gone?

Not since 1944–45
have I felt so dumbly, utterly,
in the wrong place at
entirely the wrong time,
caught then in that merciless war,

now trapped here, old, on a blossoming earth,
nose filled with burgeoning odors,
wind a caress, sound blurred reassurance,
echo of others, the lovely compacting
human warmths, the eye closing upon you,

seeing eye, sight's companion, dark or light,
makes out of its lonely distortions
it's you again, coming closer, feel
weight in the bed beside me,
close to my bones.

They told me it would be
like this but who could
believe it, not to leave, not to
go away? "I'll hate to
leave this earthly paradise..."

There's no time like the present,
no time in the present. Now it floats, goes out like a boat
upon the sea. Can't we see,
can't we now be company
to that one of us

has to go? *Hold my hand, dear.*
I should have hugged him,
taken him up, held him,
in my arms. I should
have let him know I was here.

Is it my turn now,
who's to say or wants to?
You're not sick, there are
certainly those older.
Your time will come.

In God's hands it's cold.
In the universe it's an empty, echoing silence.
Only us to make sounds,
but I made none.
I sat there like a stone.

III

LIFE & DEATH
THERE
INSIDE MY HEAD

LIFE & DEATH

If I had thought
one moment
to reorganize life
as a particular pattern,
to outwit distance, depth,
felt dark was myself
and looked for the hand
held out to me, I
presumed. It grew by itself.

•

It had seemed diligence,
a kind of determined
sincerity, just to keep going,
mattered, people would care
you were there.
I hadn't thought of death—
or anything that happened
simply because it happened.
There was no reason there.

"OH MY GOD…"

Oh my god— You
are a funny face
and your smile
thoughtful, your teeth
sharp— The agonies
of simple existence
lifted me up. But
the mirror I looked in
now looks back.

●

It wasn't God
but something else
was at the end,
I thought, would
get you like
my grandpa dead
in coffin
was gone forever,
so they said.

Out here there
is a soundless float
and the earth
seems far below—
or out. The stars
and the planets
glow on the wall.
Inside each one
we fuck, we fuck.

●

But I didn't mean to,
I didn't dare to look.
The first time couldn't
even find the hole
it was supposed to go in—
Lonely down here
in simple skin,
lonely, lonely
without you.

Sear at the center,
convoluted, tough passage,
history's knots,
the solid earth—
What streaked
consciousness, faint
design so secured
semen's spasm,
made *them*?

●

I didn't know then,
had only an avarice
to tear open
love and eat its person,
feeling confusion,
driven, wanting
inclusion, hunger
to feel, smell, taste
her flesh.

"IN THE DIAMOND..."

In the diamond
above earth,
over the vast, inchoate,
boiling *material*
plunging up, cresting
as a forming cup, on the truncated
legs of a man stretched out,
the nub of penis alert,
once again the story's told.

•

Born very young into a world
already very old, Zukofsky'd said.
I heard the jokes
the men told
down by the river, swimming.
What are you
supposed to do
and how do you learn.
I feel the same way now.

"THE LONG ROAD..."

The long road of it all
is an echo,
a sound like an image
expanding, frames growing
one after one in ascending
or descending order, all
of us a rising, falling
thought, an explosion
of emptiness soon forgotten.

•

As a kid I wondered
where do they go,
my father dead. The place
had a faded dustiness
despite the woods and all.
We all grew up.
I see our faces
in old school pictures.
Where are we now?

"WHEN IT COMES..."

When it comes,
it loses edge,
has nothing around it,
no place now present
but impulse not one's own,
and so empties into a river
which will flow on
into a white cloud
and be gone.

●

Not me's going!
I'll hang on till
last wisp of mind's
an echo, face shreds
and moldering hands,
and all of whatever
it was can't say
any more to
anyone.

THERE

Then when those shades so far from us had run
    That they could now be seen no more, arose
    A new thought in me and then another one,
And many and divers others sprang from those,
    And I so wandered in and out of them
    That all the wandering made mine eyes to close,
And thinking was transmuted into dream.

Dante, *Purgatorio*

THERE

The wall is at
        What I never said
the beginning faint
        what I couldn't touch

faces between thin
        was me in you
edges of skin
        you in me

an aching determination
        dumb sad pain
inside and out
        wasted blame

thought
        the edge I battered
feeling
        trying to get in

of places things
away from myself
they are in or are
locked in doubt

between all this
only myself
and that too again.
trying still to get out.

FEARFUL LOVE

Love was my heart
 No one cares
in the pit
 even feels

in the dark
 the stares
was my fear
 the evil

in the coil
 I screamed to myself
of the near
 turned into picture

of another where
 saw only myself
a congress of birds
 in the sullen mirror

waited to hear
 had become one of them
what a gun could say
 fixed in a form

to a simple world what the white
 abstract dead
faced one now would say.
 out of my head.

LOOP

I left it behind
    Only me
in the dark
    like they say

for others to find
    no one more
as they came in
    than another

two and two
    if there
the doubles of desire
    it's enough

their bodies' architecture
    inside flesh
myself still inside
    I could be

singing small grey bird
    more than reflection
caught by design
    fixed as an echo

upright cock breast
    be myself more
hips the rope's loop.
    like passage like door.

HAND

This way to end
    Comes too close
an outstretched hand
    to me frightens

reaches forward to find
    stuns what I feel
place for itself
    argues existence

fingers grown large
    makes me confused
in eye's disposition
    makes pattern of place

opaque dark
    textures of patience
skirt's billowing pattern
    all afterthought

there on the palm
    destructive bored
perched on finger
    else pulses behind

bird looks out
    comes forward to find
secure in its doubt.
    grabs on to my mind.

BODY

What twisting thought
    I'd been taken
holds in place
    held driven

parts of mind
    brought fixed
body's found
    displaced in reflection

makes grace weight
    love sounded
hangs head down
    included secured

stands behind puts out
    made me other
arms with their hands
    than simplifying thought

whether up or down
    broken out doubling cock
here come to rest
    head hung faceless

one and another
    down hands
at last together.
    held me held me.

INSIDE MY HEAD

INSIDE MY HEAD

Inside my head a common room,
a common place, a common tune,
a common wealth, a common doom

inside my head. I close my eyes.
The horses run. Vast are the skies,
and blue my passing thoughts' surprise

inside my head. What is this space
here found to be, what is this place
if only me? Inside my head, whose face?

First there, it proves to be still here.
Distant as seen, it comes then to be near.
I found it here and there unclear.

What if my hand had only been
extension of an outside reaching in
to work with common means to change me then?

All things are matter, yet these seem
caught in the impatience of a dream,
locked in the awkwardness they mean.

THE SWAN

Peculiar that *swan* should mean *a sound?*
I'd thought of gods and power, and wounds.
But here in the curious quiet this one has settled down.

All day the barking dogs were kept at bay.
Better than dogs, a single swan, they say,
will keep all such malignant force away

and so preserve a calm, make pond a swelling lake—
sound through the silent grove a shattering spate
of resonances, jarring the mind awake.

THE ROSE

Into one's self come in again,
here as if ever now to once again begin
with beauty's old, old problem never-ending—

Go, lovely rose... So was that story told
in some extraordinary place then, *once upon a time* so old
it seems an echo now as it again unfolds.

I point to *me* to look out at the world.
I see the white, white petals of this rose unfold.
I know such beauty in the world grows cold.

THE SKULL

"Come closer. Now there is nothing left
either inside or out to gainsay death,"
the skull that keeps its secrets saith.

The ways one went, the forms that were
empty as wind and yet they stirred
the heart to its passion, all is passed over.

Lighten the load. Close the eyes.
Let the mind loosen, the body die,
the bird fly off to the opening sky.

THE STAR

Such space it comes again to be,
a room of such vast possibility,
a depth so great, a way so free.

Life and its person, thinking to find
a company wherewith to keep the time
a peaceful passage, a constant rhyme,

stumble perforce, must lose their way,
know that they go too far to stay
stars in the sky, children at play.

INDEX OF TITLES